# The Wild Life of FROGS

By Camilla de la Bédoyère

WINDMILL BOOKS

THE WILD SIDE

Published in 2015 by **WINDMILL BOOKS**, an Imprint of Rosen Publishing
29 East 21st Street, New York, NY 10010



Publishing Director: Belinda Gallagher
Creative Director: Jo Cowan
Editorial Director: Rosie McGuire
Designer: Jo Cowan
Image Manager: Liberty Newton
Production Manager: Elizabeth Collins
Reprographics: Stephan Davis, Anthony Cambray, Thom Allaway

## Acknowledgements

The publishers would like to thank Mike Foster (Maltings Partnership), Joe Jones, and Richard Watson (Bright Agency) for the illustrations they contributed to this book. All other artwork from the Miles Kelly Artwork Bank.

The publishers would like to thank the following sources for the use of their photographs: t = top, b = bottom, l = left, r = right, c = center, bg = background, rt = repeated throughout. **Cover** (front, m) Statsenko/Shutterstock, (front, bl) EcoPrint/ Shutterstock; (back) Eric Isselée; (Joke panel) Tropinina Olga. **Corbis** 15(r) Michael & Patricia Fogden. **FLPA** 5(b) Foto Natura Stock; 10 Scott Linstead/Minden Pictures; 13 Michael & Patricia Fogden/Minden Pictures. **iStock** 8–9(bg) Ewa Mazur. **Nature Picture Library** 11(tr) Stephen Dalton. **Shutterstock** Joke panel (rt) Irzik; Heading panel (rt) cristi180884; Learn a Word panel (rt) iaRada; 1 Statsenko/Shutterstock, (front, bl) EcoPrint/Shutterstock; 4–5(m) Anneka; 5(tr) Lobke Peers; 6 Brian Lasenby; 7(l) Roger Meerts, (br) Shane Kennedy; 8(panel tr) Anna Ts, (musical notes) Tracie Andrews, (speech bubble) tachyglossus; 9(frog panel r) Okuneva Tatiana, (fruit stickers) Andra Popovici; 11(b) Eric Isselée; 12–13 Cathy Keifer; 14(t) Statsenko, (l) Stefan Fierros, (b) Matej Ziak; 15(c) Dr. Morley Read; 16(t,bg) donatas1205, (t) Stephanie Lirette, (b) LittleRambo; 17(t, bg) TinyFish, (bl) Kakigori Studio, (cr) Elena Kalistratova; 19(t) EcoPrint, (b) Statsenko; 20 worldswildlifewonders; 21(t) Eric Isselée, (b) Steve Bower.

## Library of Congress Cataloging-in-Publication Data

De la Bédoyère, Camilla, author.
The wild life of frogs / Camilla de la Bedoyere.
pages cm. — (The wild side)
Includes index.
ISBN 978-1-4777-5519-8 (pbk.)
ISBN 978-1-4777-5520-4 (6 pack)
ISBN 978-1-4777-5518-1 (library binding)
1. Frogs—Juvenile literature. 2. Amphibians—Juvenile literature. I. Title.
QL668.E2D45 2015
597.8—dc23

2014027100

Manufactured in the United States of America

CPSIA Compliance Information: Batch #CW15WM: For Further Information contact Rosen Publishing, New York, New York at 1-800-237-9932

# Contents

# What are you?

Large eyes

## I am a frog!

I am a kind of animal called an amphibian. Amphibians can live in water and on land. We lay eggs and like living in wet places.

There are more than 5,000 different types of frogs!

**Q.** What's the difference between a cat and a frog?

**A.** A cat has nine lives but a frog croaks every night.

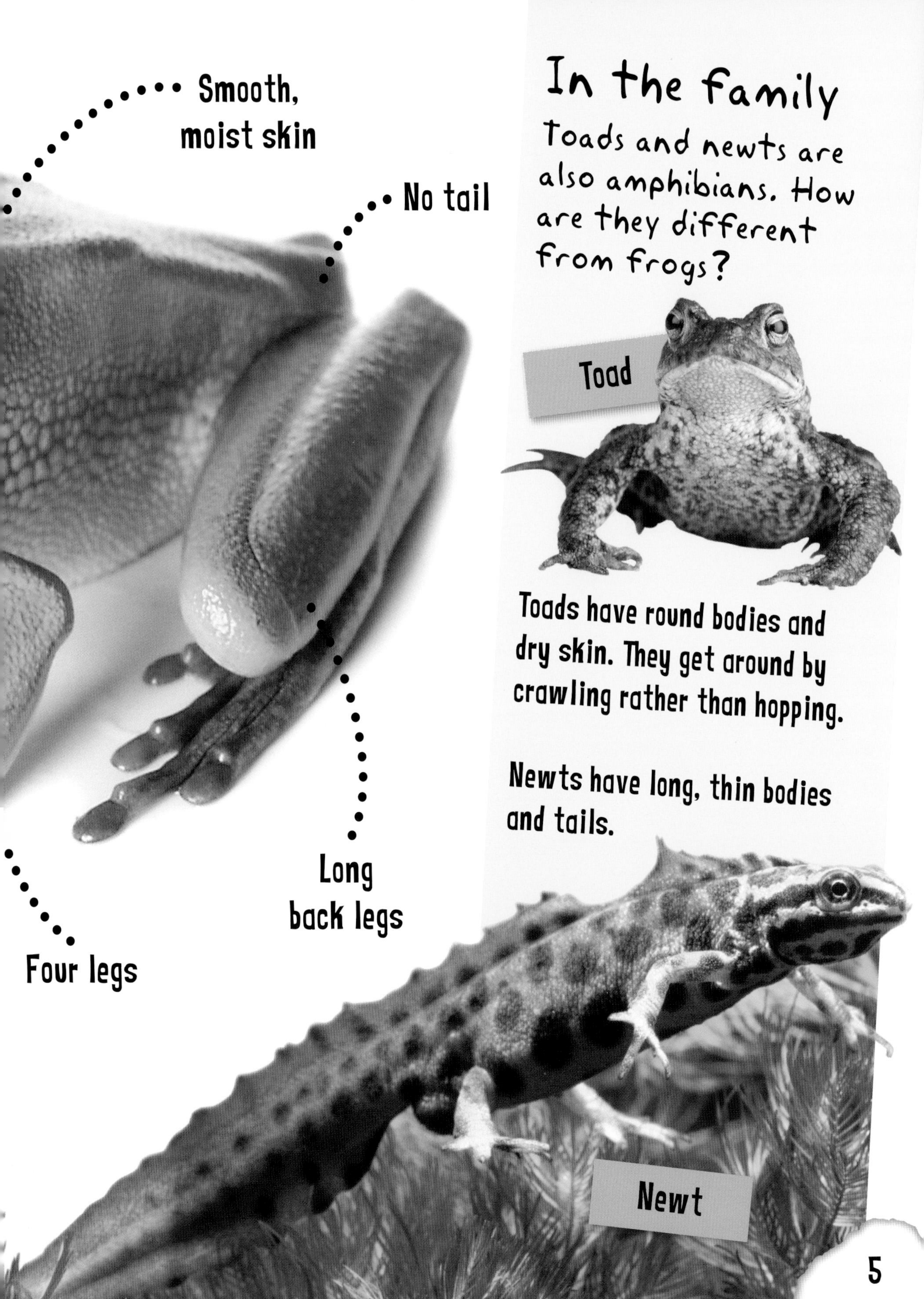


# In the family

Toads and newts are also amphibians. How are they different from frogs?

Toads have round bodies and dry skin. They get around by crawling rather than hopping.

Newts have long, thin bodies and tails.

# Where do you live?

I live on the ground.

My skin is green and brown to help me hide under plants. I stay near water because my skin has to be moist.

## Sticky!

Some frogs live in trees. They have sticky pads on their toes that help them to climb.

**Q.** What is green and slimy and found at the North Pole?

**A.** A lost frog!

## Keeping warm

Some frogs have a winter sleep called hibernation. They hide under rocks or leaves and don't come out until spring.

# Activity time

## Get ready to make and do!

### Croaky contest

Which of your friends can make the best frog noise? Give points for the most realistic, silliest, loudest, and croakiest.

### Draw me!

YOU WILL NEED: pencils · paper

1. Draw two squashed circles to make your frog's head and body.

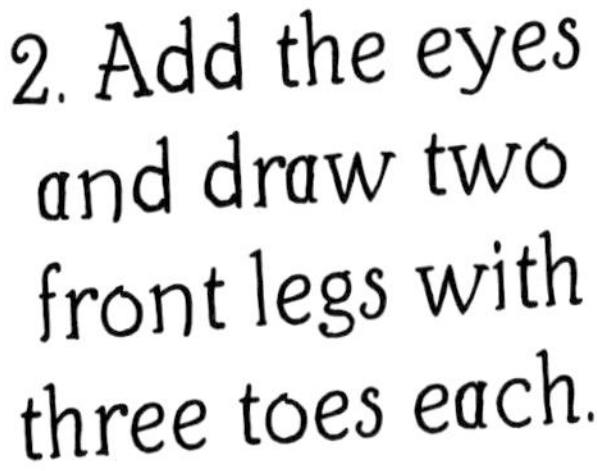

2. Add the eyes and draw two front legs with three toes each.

3. Give your frog back legs and a wide mouth.

Now color me in and give me a name!

Ask for help!

# Handy frog

## YOU WILL NEED:

paper plate · green paint
paintbrush · white paper or thin card stock
scissors · black felt-tip pen · sticky tape

## HERE'S HOW:

1. Paint one side of the plate green and leave to dry.
2. Make two green handprints on a piece of paper or card stock and leave to dry.
3. Cut out the handprints and tape them to the back of the plate.
4. Cut two "eyes" from the paper or card stock and tape at the top of the plate.
5. Draw the frog's features with the pen.

# Yummy green smoothie

## YOU WILL NEED:

2 peeled kiwis
1 peeled frozen banana
½ cup vanilla yogurt
a splash of milk
1 tsp honey
a few drops of green food coloring

## HERE'S HOW:

Put all the ingredients into a blender and blend until smooth. Serve in a chilled glass. Delicious!

# How far can you jump?

## I can jump a long way!

I jump to get away from animals that might eat me. The African sharp-nosed frog can jump 16 feet (4.9 m) in one giant leap!

# Flying frogs

Frogs don't have wings, but some seem to fly. They leap from trees and glide to the ground.

# Super swimmers

All frogs have long legs and most have webbed feet to help them swim fast.

# What do you eat?

## I love to eat bugs!

But I will eat almost anything I can catch. I gobble up spiders, worms, slugs, snails, and even small fish.

## Fast food

Good eyesight helps a frog to spot bugs. Then its long tongue shoots out to catch them.

Frogs don't chew their food – they don't have any teeth!

## A mouthful of mouse

A horned frog can catch a mouse or lizard and swallow it in one gulp!

## Down it goes

When a frog swallows food it rolls its eyes. The eyes move down and help push the food into the frog's throat!

# What are your babies called?

My babies are called tadpoles.

Frog

1

The eggs are called frogspawn and frogs lay them in water, in springtime.

The eggs hatch and little tadpoles swim out. They have tails and live in water.

2

## Super dad

Most frogs do not look after their babies. They lay eggs and swim away before they hatch.

Froglet

3

The tadpoles grow legs, and their tails shrink. They become froglets, and can leave the water.

This tree frog dad is carrying two baby tadpoles on his back.

**LEARN A WORD:**

**metamorphosis**

The change in body shape that happens during some animals' lives.

# Puzzle time

## Can you solve all the puzzles?

### Tell us apart

There are three differences between Freddie and Frank – can you spot them?

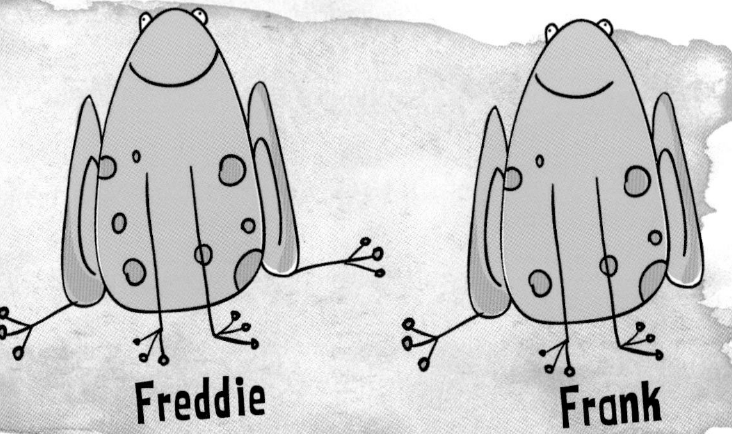


### True or false?

1. A baby frog is called a tadpool.
2. Bullfrogs bellow when they are talking to their friends.
3. Frogs like living in wet places.

**ANSWERS: 1.** False – it is called a tadpole **2.** False – they bellow to attract a mate **3.** True.

### Rhyme time

Only four of these words rhyme with "frog." Can you find them?

dog fade fog four
pig pond log
mug clog splash

**ANSWER:** dog, fog, log, clog

## Count me in

Felix the frog usually eats ten spiders every day. One day Felix gives away half of his spiders to a hungry friend. How many spiders does Felix have left?

ANSWER: 5

## Who caught the fly?

Which of these frogs has caught a fly with her long, sticky tongue? Trace with your finger to find out.



ANSWER: Florence

# What noise do you make?

## I make a very loud noise!

Frogs make lots of noises. We can croak, ribbit, sing, twitter, click, and chirp.

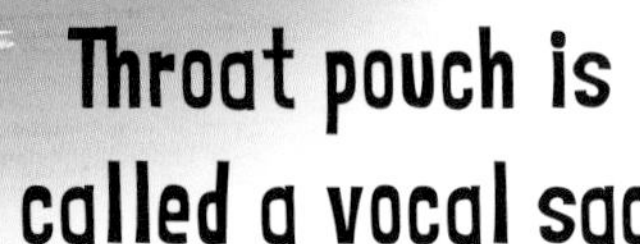

**Q.** What is a frog's favorite type of music?

**A.** Hip-hop!

## Frog chorus

Male bullfrogs are large frogs with big vocal sacs. They make deep bellowing sounds to attract females.

**LEARN A WORD:**

**pouch**

Part of an animal's body that is shaped like a bag or pocket.

## I'm over here!

Male frogs make sounds to tell females where to find them. The sounds also tell other males to stay away.

**Large ears detect sounds well**

# How do you stay safe?

## I look scary!

My bright skin lets other animals know I am dangerous to eat. Birds, lizards, and snakes eat frogs, but they stay away from me.

Poison dart frog

**LEARN A WORD:**

**poisonous**

Poisonous animals and plants are dangerous to eat or touch.

## Don't eat me!

If a hungry animal gets too close to a fire-bellied toad the toad will flash its red belly, hoping to scare it away.

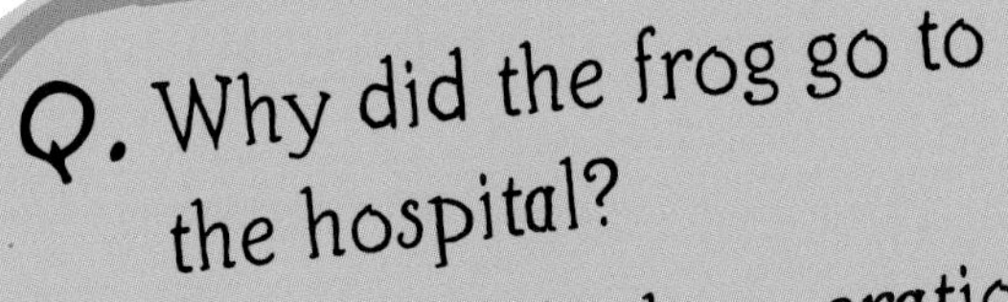


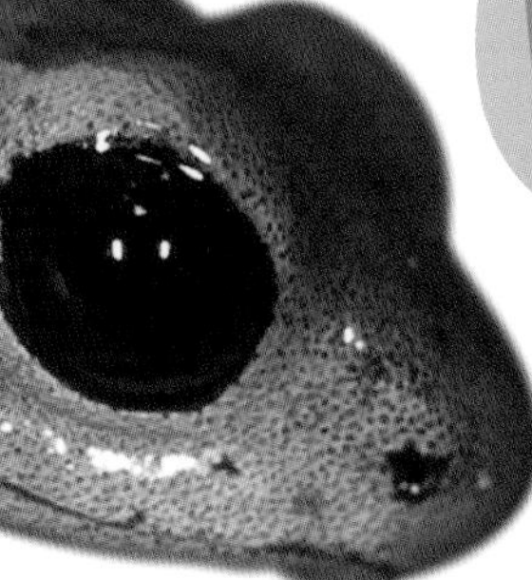

## Can you see me?

This frog is trying to hide inside a flower. Do you think the color of its skin helps it to "disappear?"

# The frog prince

**Once upon a time,** there was a rude and spoiled princess. One day she was playing with her ball in the garden. She threw it high in the air, and it landed with a splash in the well. The princess was angry. She kicked the side of the well and a large frog plopped out. Then the frog spoke – it croaked, "Why are you making so much noise?"

The princess ordered the frog to fetch her ball. The frog leapt down the well and returned with the ball, but when the princess went to snatch it, the frog said, "Hasn't anyone taught you any manners? I have a request: I want to come and live in the palace, and eat off your plate, and sleep on your pillow, please."

The princess thought a promise to a frog wouldn't count, so she agreed. She took her ball and ran back to the palace. But her father the king said she must keep her word.

The princess sulked. She refused to eat her dinner with the frog sitting beside her. When bedtime came, she carried him to her

room by one leg. She only let the frog sleep on the edge of her bed, while she did not sleep a wink all night.

On the second evening the princess ate nothing again, and once more she did not sleep.

On the third night the princess was hungry, so she ate up all her dinner. At bedtime she was so tired that she fell deeply asleep.

The next morning the princess woke to find a handsome prince standing at the foot of her bed. He told her that a fairy had turned him into a frog because he was spoiled. The spell could only be broken if someone just as rude was nice to him.

The princess learned her lesson, and from that day forward she was much nicer. Before long, the princess and the prince were married and they lived happily ever after.

A retelling from the original story by the Brothers Grimm

# Glossary

**amphibian** an animal (such as a frog or toad) that can live both on land and in water

**bellow** a deep roaring shout or sound

**croak** a deep hoarse sound made by a frog

**glide** to move or float with a smooth continuous motion, typically with little noise

**gulp** swallow (drink or food) quickly or in large mouthfuls

**hibernation** passing the winter in a sleeping or resting state

**manners** a person's way of behaving toward others

**moist** slightly wet or damp

**newt** a small, slender-bodied amphibian with a well-developed tail

**webbed** having toes that are connected

# Websites

For web resources related to the subject of this book, go to:
**www.windmillbooks.com/weblinks**
and select this book's title.

# Index